Josep Lluís

SERT

ROCKPORT

Josep Lluís

SERT

GLOUCESTER MASSACHUSETTS

ROCKPORT PUBLISHERS

Editor: Sofía Cheviakoff

Texts: Sofía Cheviakoff, (page 14, 22, 66, Alberto Duarte)

Graphic Design: Emma Termes Parera

Layout: Soti Mas-Bagà

Translation: William Bain

Copyright for the international edition:

© H Kliczkowski-Onlybook, S.L.

La Fundición, 15. Polígono Industrial Santa Ana

28529 Rivas-Vaciamadrid. Madrid

Ph.: +34 91 666 50 01

Fax: +34 91 301 26 83

asppan@asppan.com

www.onlybook.com

Copyright for the U.S. edition:

© 2003 by Rockport Publishers, Inc.

Published in the United States of America by

Rockport Publishers, Inc.

33 Commercial Street

Gloucester, Massachusetts 01930-5089

Telephone: (978) 282-9590

Fax: (978) 283-2742

www.rockpub.com

Library of Congress Cataloging-in-Publication Data available

ISBN: 1-56496-985-1

10 9 8 7 6 5 4 3 2 1

Printed in China

Josep Lluís Sert (1902-1983) was born into a well-off Catalan family related to the world of art. These early connections with artistic activities brought Sert into contact with artists from the time of his early childhood, thus establishing an intellectual basis on which he would draw when he began to study architecture.

Sert had barely begun his university studies in Barcelona when he made a trip to a Paris. There, he collaborated closely with Le Corbusier and Pierre Jeanneret. It was on this sojourn in the French capital that the young Sert first spent time with Picasso, Miró, and Calder, among other artists, joining in long conversations on the arts, architecture, and the common ground among the different disciplines. At that time, it was habitual practice to commission an artist of known prestige with an architectural project, and Sert managed to develop design into a joint process, a close collaboration involving the client, the architect, and the artist.

The influence of Le Corbusier on Sert is clearly a reinterpretation of Mediterranean architecture: the brise-soleil—as a kind of revitalizing of the wall, the building taken into its own self-reflection, turned to the inside as a place of repose and introspection—in short, the patio house. Buildings like Sert's own in Cambridge, the Presidential Palace in Cuba, the United States Embassy in Iraq, Joan Miró's studio in Palma de Mallorca, Spain, the Miró Foundation in Barcelona or the Maeght Foundation in Saint Paul-de-Vence, France.

The treatment of light is another fundamental aspect in the architecture Sert developed. The highly characteristic skylights that adorn his pieces, such as the Miró Foundation, or the Faculty Library (Boston University), are elements that capture the natural light and reflect it indirectly, diffusing it through the building's interior.

His enterprising spirit led him to participate actively in almost every congress of the International Congress of Modern Architecture (Spanish acronym, CIAM), and he was even elected president of the Eighth

Congress. The subject of these meetings was usually centered around the development and reconstruction of cities, a topic of growing importance due to the ravages that had been caused by the two wars that shook Europe in the first half of the twentieth century.

In 1945, now already established in New York, Sert associated himself with Paul Lester Wiener and Paul Schultz to form the Town Planning Associates. The associates received many commissions for city development plans for South American cities. There, however, they were faced with social features—marginality and poverty—and climates that were highly distinct from those of the United States. They carried out projects in the Cidade des Motores (Brasil) and Chimbote (Peru), where they applied their new formulas for adapting the structure to the environment. They thus managed to surpass the dogmas of modern urbanism with its proposals of a universalist architecture. They followed the directive plans of Medellín and of Bogotá and the pilot plan of La Habana. For the 15 years in which he lived in the city of the skyscrapers, Sert met and made friends with many artists like Mondrian, Duchamp, Masson, Max Ernst, and Tanguy.

In 1953, Josep Lluís Sert was named dean of the Graduate School of Design at Harvard, substituting Walter Gropius, and head of studies in the Department of Architecture of the same institution. He did not, however, abandon his tasks in the New York offices. Some of his projects from this period were commissioned by Harvard University and Boston University; others were large works like that on Roosevelt Island and Riverview, both in New York. The following year, he moved to Cambridge, Massachusetts, where he joined Huson Jackson to found Sert, Jackson & Associates.

In the mid-1970s, Sert returned to Spain, where he did projects like the studio for his close friend Joan Miró in Palma de Mallorca, the precursor of his commission for the Maeght Foundation and the Miró Foundation. Ibiza, the city that had so inspired creation in the 1930s, received one of Sert's most emblematic works, the Punta Martinet houses.

This complex is on a strategic site between the main campus of Harvard University and the student residence halls. This particular placement made it easier for the zone to channel much of the pedestrian traffic between these two areas. The center occupies a full block of Massachusetts Avenue between Holyoke Street and Dunster Street. Its construction replaced more than 20 buildings on the site. It was raised in two phases: the first ended in 1962, and the second in 1966. The building is highly versatile, with a large commercial mall on the ground floor and numerous university administration departments on the upper floors. Additionally, Holyoke Center houses the university medical center.

On the ground floor are the information office, a bank, a press office, 20 stores, and a University Health Service pharmacy. At one end of the gallery is a small garden; at the other end is a brick plaza that has chess tables offering games in the shade of the trees.

In the words of Sert himself, "The building is framed in cast-in-place concrete columns and waffle slabs, with gray precast concrete infill panels, transparent glass and translucent glass, a system that conserves energy while allowing varied partition arrangements inside... Interior spaces are planned with brightly colored fabrics and wall surfaces that emphasize the architecture of the building. Furnishings were specially designed to the client's requirements. Natural sunlight enters the building through the skylights at key locations."

In a refurbishment project recently carried out, the mall needed to be closed off with glass to avoid the formation of air currents, and the lighting systems were modernized. At present, there are restaurants, spaces for exhibiting art, many, many shops, and information points about the university. It is one of the meeting places that visitors to Harvard most want to get to know.

Architects: Sert, Jackson & Associates
Address: Harvard University, Cambridge, Massachusetts, USA
Area: 309,407 sq. ft.
Construction Date: 1958-1966
Photography: Michael Hamilton

Typical plan

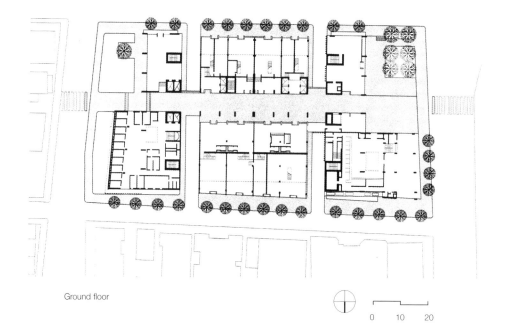

Ground floor

0   10   20

In spite of the project's large dimensions, the spaces maintain a human scale. The variety available in the mall spaces on the ground floor make the building a much-used social center and entertainment center for Harvard's students and also for the residents of Cambridge. Sert also drew up plans for the surroundings of the buildings, the paving, the parterres, and the vegetation to be planted around the site.

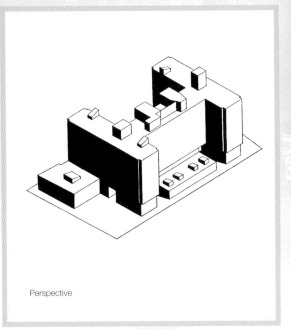

Perspective

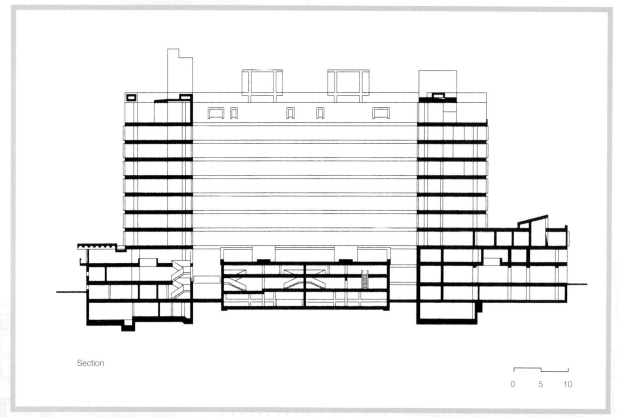

Section

0   5   10

The Margueritte and Aimé Maeght Foundation was born as a challenge to integrate all of the plastic arts in a single building. Some of the artists represented by Maeght were old friends who Sert had known in París, and this constituted an opportunity to actually put into effect some of the ideas that had come out of their conversations in the cafés during the 1930s.

The location on a hill with no small number of pine trees, a privileged climate and a singular view make the Alps and the Cap d'Antibes certain to play very important roles in outdoor spaces.

The project rejects out of hand the idea of a singular structure and chooses to work on a scale more closely suitable to the surroundings: spaces and volumes are linked as they would be in a small town. Not only the gardens but the patios as well spring up in areas that have been specially prepared for the exposition. The artists represented by the foundation contribute with works conceived with these zones in mind so that, additionally, a close link has already been achieved in their very conception.

The whole amounts to a series of different buildings joined together by means of outdoor squares and paths. Three elements play very key roles here, in addition to a small chapel and the caretaker's house. The largest piece, in the eastern zone (which includes a more recent extension with an auditorium seating 600 people), has a single ceiling height and uses to good advantage the difference in grade to establish its two levels. It houses the permanent galleries containing work by the artists Georges Braque, Joan Miró, Marc Chagall, and Vassily Kandinsky. It also contains a gallery for temporary shows. The treatment of indirect lighting is effected largely by way of the large skylights. These elements also infuse rhythm and scale into the work. A vestibule provides the interface between this gallery and another building characterized essentially by the large inverted arches that form its roof.

This four-story structure contains a large hall that is used both for conferences and exhibits and also includes a library. It is located at the western entrance, and from this point it works as a visual separator for the different parts of the complex. Lastly, the director's residence, on the western side, was raised with rubble walls like all of the other walls in the complex.

Collaborators: Bellini, Lizero and Gozzi
Location: Saint-Paul-de-Vence, France
Construction Date: 1959-1964
Photography: Roger Casas

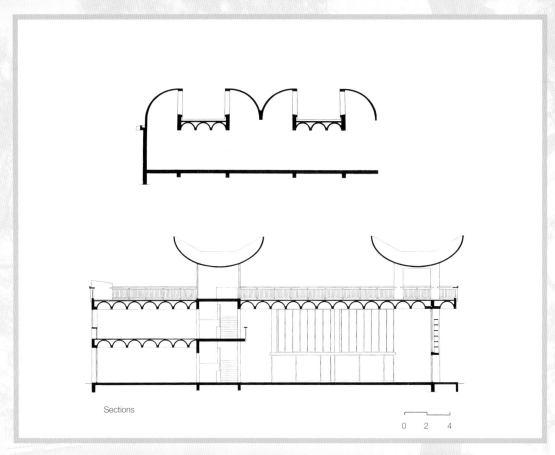

Sections

0 2 4

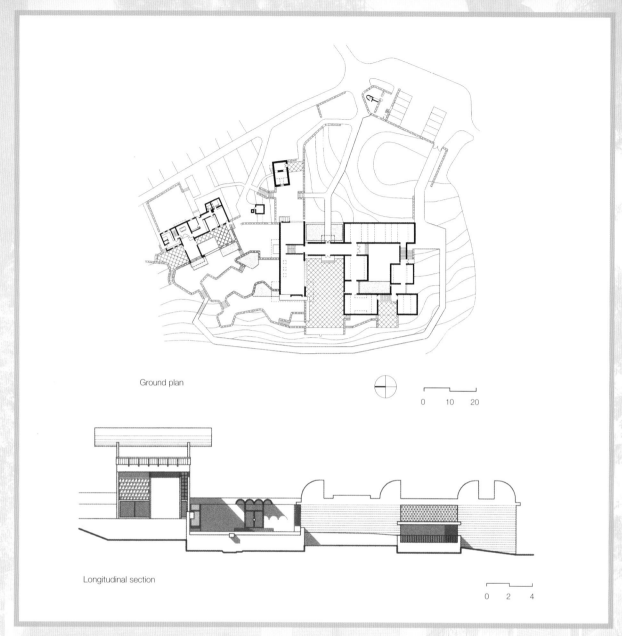

Ground plan

0   10   20

Longitudinal section

0   2   4

This project for apartments for married students at Harvard University arose out of the need the educational institution felt to integrate, as part of the learning process and in a location with some proximity to the main campus, the students' and instructors' extracurricular activities in an ever-changing exchange environment. The block was thus designed starting from the premise that it should promote communication and a metacentric community spirit among its inhabitants. To this effect, the complex does its best to interface with the exterior gardens and plazas where community activities take place.

Sited on the shores of the River Charles, Peabody Terrace contains, with parking included, blocks of three, five, and seven stories. They respectfully adapt to the scale of their surroundings, made up basically of medium-height Georgian style buildings, these also being destined for use as student housing. To maximize space as well as to manage a density of 203 dwellings per hectare (2.47 acres), the design establishes three svelte 22-floor towers, each carefully linked to a given group of blocks.

Architects: Sert, Jackson & Gourley
Location: Harvard University, Cambridge,
Massachusetts, USA
Construction Date: 1962-1964
Photography: Michael Hamilton

The circulation system begins with a pedestrian esplanade. This is the vertebral column of the set of buildings: in addition to acting as nexus for the rest of the neighborhood and the river, it promotes the desired development of the community spaces and the entrances to each building.

Not only the towers but also the rest of the buildings have an independent circulation grid, i.e., elevators and stairs and hallways, respectively. But, in line with the awareness of the concept of community integration, the top floor of each block is connected by a towered bridge, and this is what runs the mixed-system program that subtends the whole project.

In order to make the project cost effective, the architects established a basic module of six apartments that join with each other by way of a corridor every three floors. This made it possible to mass-produce the necessary elements for the building. This system is used both in the blocks and in the towers. Adding or subtracting pieces then generates different rooms and achieves variety in height and given spatial qualities, fenestration, and accessways.

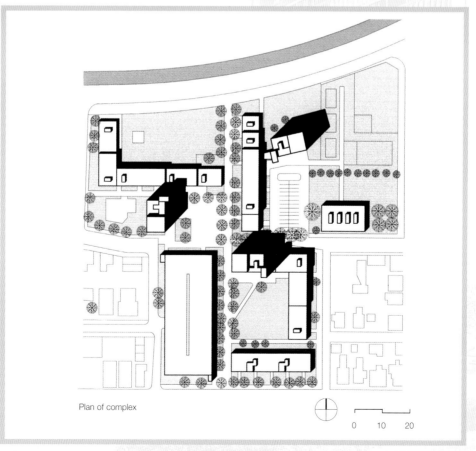

Plan of complex

0   10   20

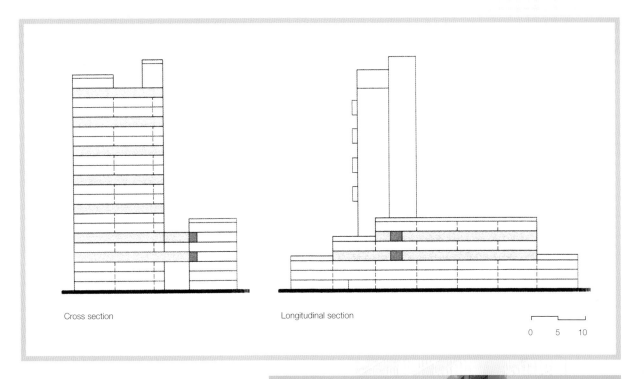

Cross section

Longitudinal section

0   5   10

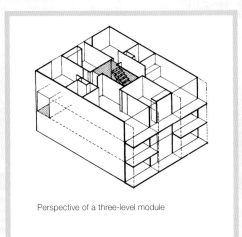

Perspective of a three-level module

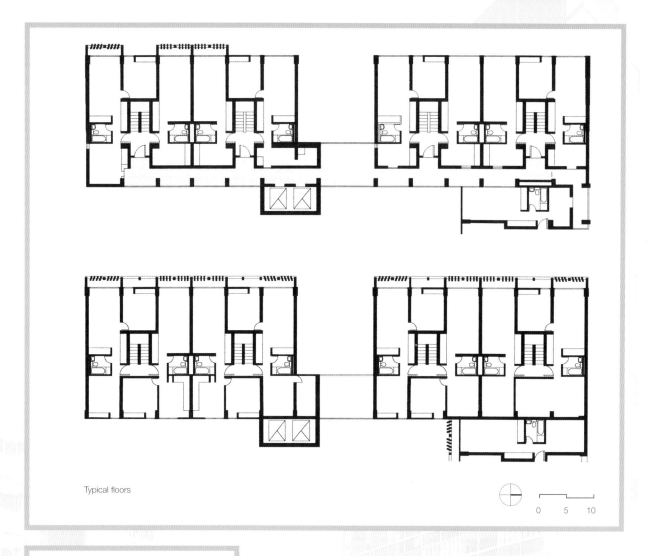

Typical floors

0   5   10

The exteriors were carefully designed to create agreeable spaces where community activities could be developed and enjoyed. The terraces are all easily accessible and they are gardened spaces.

When Boston University decided to concentrate all of its faculties on a single central campus, a terrain was chosen on the Charles River in the center of the City of Boston. The in-no-way generous dimensions of this location made it necessary to design a complex of great density.

The problem of population density was solved by using a high-rise tower. The decision was also made to orient the whole to face the river and thus take advantage of the beauty of the landscape.

The commission included the planning of a student center, the Mugar Library, and the Law and Education Departments. The law library and the auditorium were built beside the high-rise towers, in a medium-height building that connected to it. Both the new structures and the already existing pieces were studied as parts of the same complex because of their proximity and their size. The distribution of all of these buildings includes exterior plazas and a large central space as interface between the old and the new.

Each building was designed as part of an urban whole. No piece would be seen as signifying in freestanding form. The volumes, and textures would not be the same if isolated on a larger site with large spaces intervening.

The student center, oriented to the northeast, has cornices on its uppermost floors. Its two air-conditioning and mechanical equipment towers give a certain perpendicularity that breaks up the long lines that follow the horizon. A central patio is in use when the climate allows. This extends the interior bays and serves as a place to display sculptures. It is the nerve center of the Student Center per se.

Mugar Library has been given a similar expression to that used in the Student Center. This time, however, the piece is turned and set back from the central plaza.

The perpendicular law and matching education dominate the whole. The fifth floor has an amphitheater with a double-height ceiling. This large space expresses itself in windowless surfaces and a style change in the jutting bodies of the tower façades.

The law library and the auditorium are in the lowest body, the building connecting the tower by way of a bridge on the second floor.

Collaborators: Hoyle, Doran and Berry; Edwin T. Steffian
Location: Boston, Massachusetts, USA
Construction Date: 1963-1966
Photography: Michael Hamilton

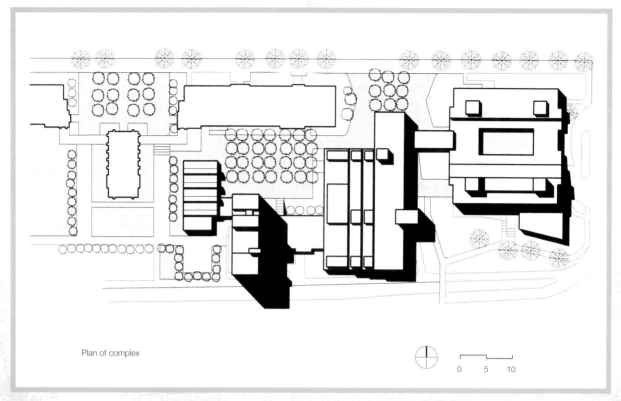

Plan of complex

0 5 10

The tower of the law and the education faculties combine windowless surfaces of concrete in the classrooms with square fenestration that provides natural lighting to offices and meeting rooms. The building containing the library and the auditorium has a skylight system that diffuses light uniformly in the interior.

Law and Education Tower

Ground floor

0 5 10

Third floor

Sixth floor

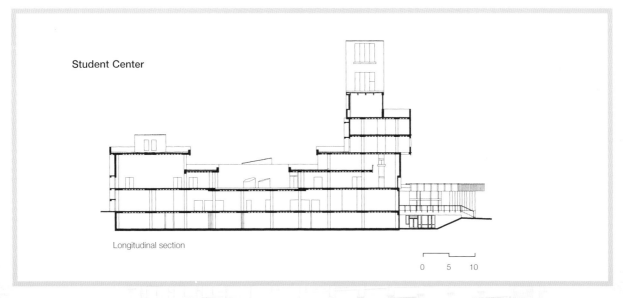

Student Center

Longitudinal section

0   5   10

The Student Center contains all university services such as dining rooms, meeting rooms, classrooms, teachers' rooms, and even small businesses. One of main objectives was to create an open building intensely related to the surrounding exterior. Thus, spaces like the cafeteria or the exhibition room lead right out to the central patio, which becomes a very busy meeting place when inclement whether doesn't keep people inside.

Student Center

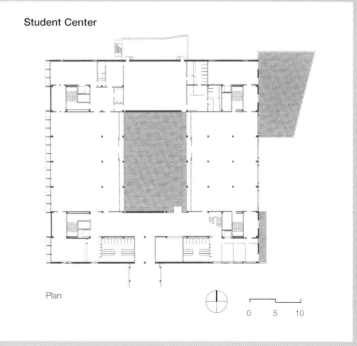

Plan

0   5   10

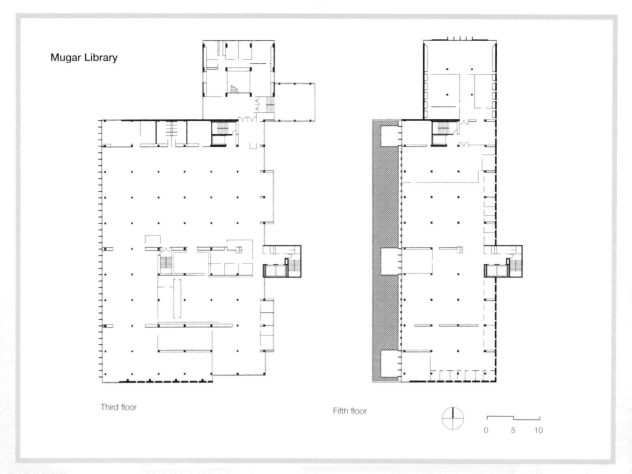

Mugar Library

Third floor

Fifth floor

0 5 10

Mugar Library was finished in 1966. It has a capacity for a million and a half books and 2,300 readers, who may occupy its different reading rooms. Different style spaces were created, some very open and well lighted, with comfortable armchairs for reading, and others more private, where it is possible to study without noise pollution.

The urbanization at Punta Martinet is on a hillside with very beautiful views of Ibiza Bay. It was designed by Sert between 1965 and 1968 and is made up of nine houses. These were built for the use of different families, and the architect conceived original designs to fit the needs of each particular client as well as the topography of the site itself.

So as to take maximum advantage of the panoramas, the structures were linked to follow the slope of the terrain, whose differences in grade were used to generate distinct patios and terraces. These then act as intermediary spaces between the interior and the exterior. The use of a system of module sizes and the reiterated use of certain exterior architectural components establishes a visual connection among all of the pieces in spite of their differences in distribution. This particular style of interfacing the houses is used because of the absence of dividing walls between each dwelling and also because of the original rubble walls natural to the island. The result obtained is a perception of the whole as a little town whose houses share an immediate heritage with the popular Mediterranean architecture of the area. Each piece is a part that fits into the whole, which in turn is developed through a unifying plastic language.

In order to tone down the intense luminosity enjoyed by this Mediterranean area, the windows, with the exception of the apertures of the terraces and balconies, have been dwarfed. Pergolas were then installed, with fixed joists of solid wood overhead, thus creating cool and agreeable ambiences with suggestive plays of light and shade.

Collaborators: Germán Rodríguez Arias, Manuel Font, Joaquín Font
Location: Ibiza, Balearic Islands, Spain
Construction Date: 1968
Photography: Pere Planells

Situation plan

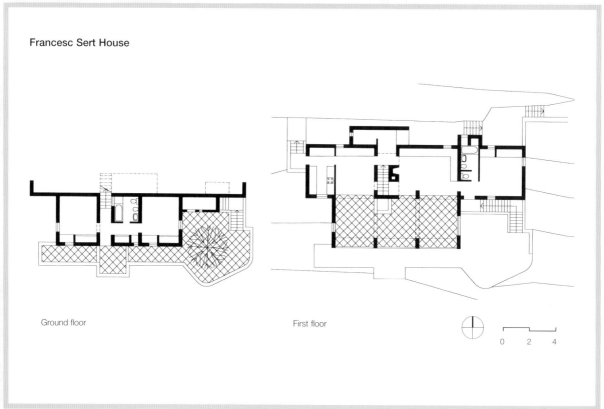

Francesc Sert House

Ground floor

First floor

0   2   4

The house of Francesc Sert occupies an arrangement that parallels the slope of the terrain. The ground floor of he houses places the day rooms and the terraces on the south side and the accessway on the north side. The bedrooms are on the first floor and here, as in the rest of the houses of Punta Martinet, most of the furniture is of masonry. Each house owner may then decorate the built-in elements in the style that suits his or her own taste.

Francesc Sert House

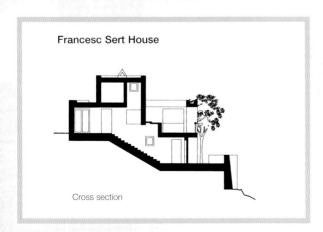

Cross section

J. Lluís Sert House

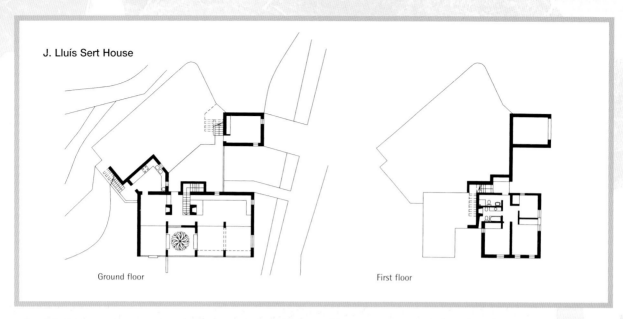

Ground floor

First floor

Sert made one of the Punta Martinet houses into his own private residence. Completely open to the sea (which, in this case, is to say its main rooms are accessed right from the Mediterranean), it comprises a set of volumes grouped together around a swimming pool that constitutes the highest point on the part of the slope on which it is sited.

J. Lluís Sert House

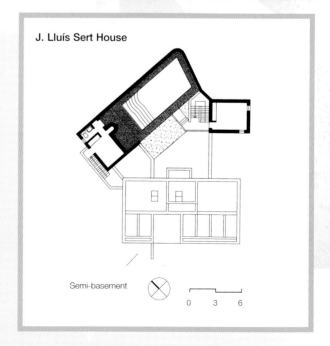

Semi-basement

0   3   6

This house emerges out of two main boxes, one being a single story with two bays and two terraces, the other a duplex containing the two bedrooms. In keeping with the way Sert had intended to conserve elements used in the traditions of this geographical zone, an old water tank now carries out the role of swimming pool. The façades combine the zone's typical whitewashing with ochre shades—still another form of blending the buildings into the landscape.

Valls House

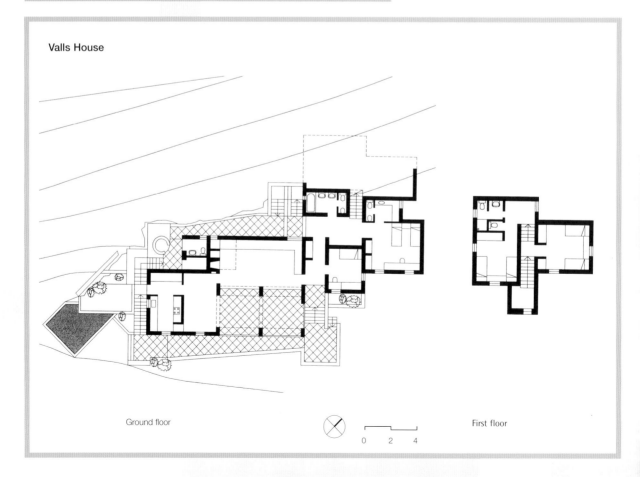

Ground floor

First floor

0   2   4

Gomis House

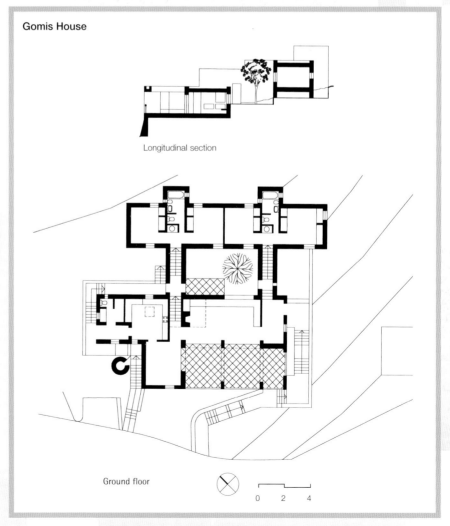

Longitudinal section

Gomis House is organized around a patio flanked by two staircases. At the highest point of the terrain, a rectangular surface area receives the bedrooms and their corresponding service areas. Downstairs, an analogous area has been used for two dayrooms, the living room and the dining room with kitchen, which includes a wide terrace.

Ground floor

0   2   4

Jutta House

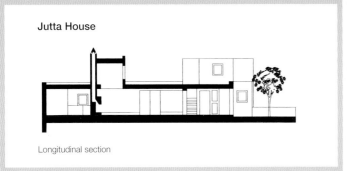

Longitudinal section

Here, the expansion of terrace is developed as a logical prolongation of the interior, a protected zone where the wash of the sun is kept off and which offers handsome views of the bay. It also protects the over-sized dining room window from the strong solar rays. It is a space that folds in on itself at the corner to assure privacy to its inhabitants. Beside the fireplace, a skylight provides overhead lighting for the living room.

Jutta House

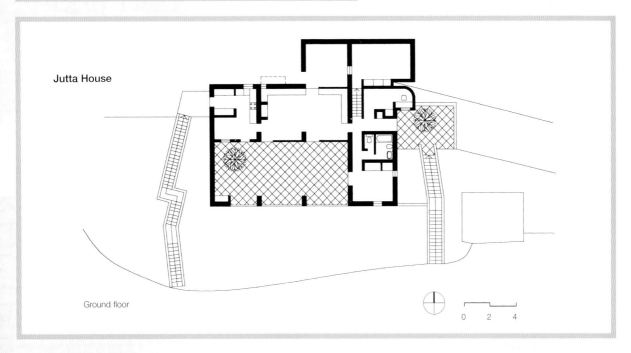

Ground floor

0   2   4

This is Harvard's largest building, 299,775 square feet in area, 145.28 feet high, and 400 feet long in its longest wing. Its nine floors and semi-basement house laboratories with a capacity for more than 800 students and five conference rooms with a seating capacity for more than 500 people.

The center was designed to house the departments of biology, geology, chemistry, physics, and mathematics, with their respective classrooms and seminars. Additionally, it contains the Cabot Science Library and a cafeteria. It is located between North and South Campus at the crossroads of pedestrian paths that make up most of the complex's internal traffic.

A rectangular mass of six floors that contains the laboratories forms a T with another set-back volume. To the west is the auditorium, which is on a half-moon plan, and to the east are two lower-height volumes that contain the library and classrooms and offices. These structures then configure a patio where the cafeteria is located.

The auditorium roof is suspended from enormous steel girders that are exposed to view on the outside. The set-back piece, perhaps the most characteristic of the entire structure, diminishes its surface area on plan as the building rises in height. The Astrology Department is on the top floor, and is fitted with a large dome-roofed observatory.

The building's frame is made of pre-stressed concrete. It was designed to allow for quick dismantling. The lengthy six-floor module contains the air-conditioning installations for most of the campus, housed in the basement and on the sixth floor.

A subterranean corridor on the southeastern side of the complex connects this area with the north side of the university, where most of the science buildings are. It also contributes to cutting down on conflicts between vehicular and pedestrian traffic and surrounds the building with a gardened zone.

Sert, Jackson & Associates won an American Institute of Architecture award for this building.

Architects: Sert, Jackson & Associates
Location: Cambridge, Massachusetts, USA
Construction Date: 1970-1972
Photography: Michael Hamilton

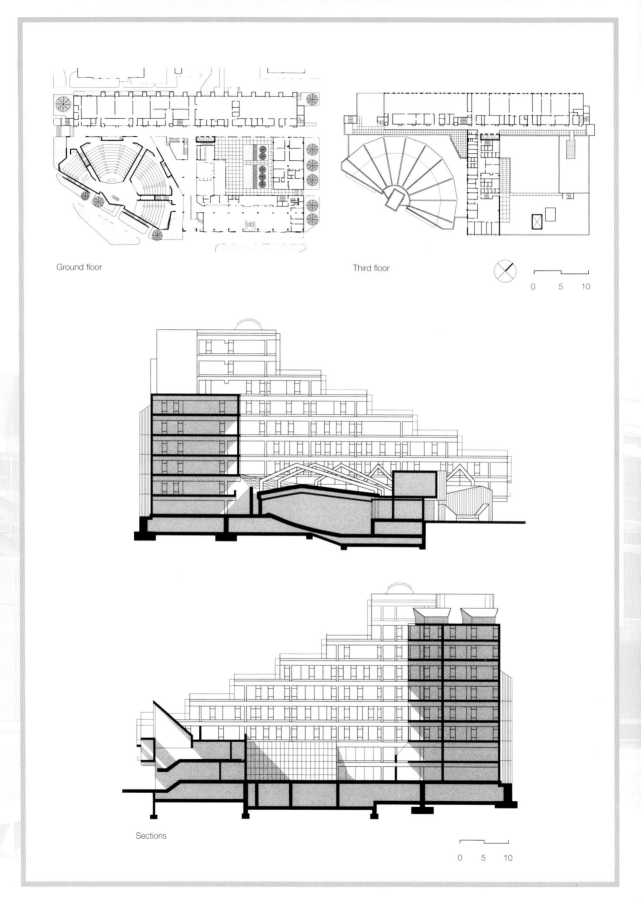

Ground floor

Third floor

0 5 10

Sections

0 5 10

The Miró Foundation was planned for the purpose of disseminating the work of the artist Joan Miró, who donated a large part of his work to the city of Barcelona. A second aim was to provide a space for the permanent exhibition of other artists on a rotating exchange basis. Additionally, the institution supports a study center that is open to researchers and to young artists.

From its privileged emplacement on a site on Montjuïc Hill, commanding an excellent view of the city of Barcelona, the complex also includes a beautiful garden facing west.

The configuration of the building—with its large skylights in curved stone, periscope-like elements, which create an aesthetic rhythm and scale—is organized around three patios. The paths around the building, parallel to these patios, confer a certain continuity to the exposition.

The ground floor of the foundation is accessed by way of a ramp that links it with one of the patios. A second ramp that runs parallel to the sculpture gallery, the only double-height room, provides access to the first floor. This upper level, with a surface area that is smaller only to that of the ground floor, gives onto a terrace that serves also as a sculpture patio and a balcony. The skylights themselves are perceived, from this terrace, like sculptural objects that frame the panoramic views.

The main building is joined by another structure, octagonal in plan and designed for administrative activities. It is a body that includes a library, an archive, and an auditorium. It communicates with the rest of the complex by way of a vertical circulation system that allows the octagon to maintain its autonomy.

The Foundation's scale, of human proportion, was created through the repetition of elements and the texture of the undressed concrete. The use of a modular system brings an intrinsic visual order to the whole building.

In 1988, the Foundation was extended in a very respectful intervention by Jaume Freixa i Janáriz, a collaborator of Sert's.

Architects: Sert, Jackson & Associates
Collaborators: J. Zalewski, Jaume Freixa i Janáriz (extension)
Location: Barcelona, Spain
Construction Date: 1975
Photography: Ferran Freixa, Jordi Miralles

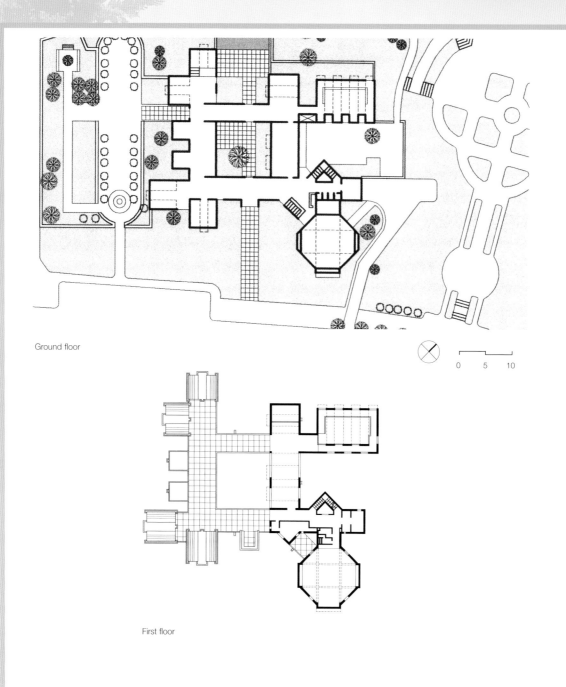

Ground floor

0   5   10

First floor

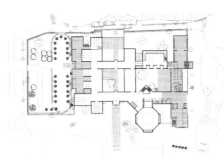

Extension sketch

The perimeter walls of the piece comprise an uninterrupted support element for the exhibition of works of art. The visitor thus has no need to return over the same route.

The entry ramp to the first floor may be read as growing out of the sculpture room and facilitating viewing access to the work on display from different points of view.

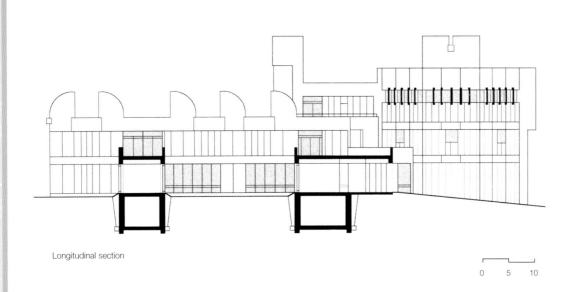

Longitudinal section

0   5   10

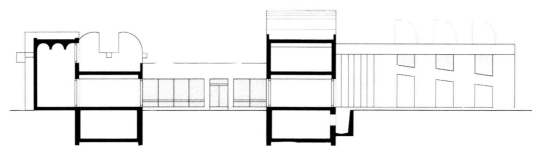

Longitudinal section

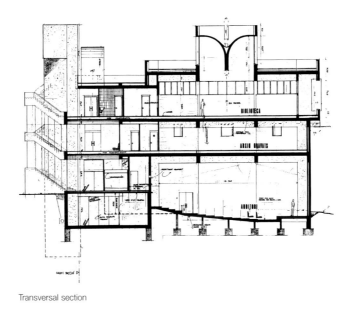

Transversal section

Joan Miró acquired an old farmhouse in Palma de Mallorca located on the side of a hill with terraced agricultural plots. This type of house, characteristic of this part of the Mediterranean, is one of low walls made of rough-hewn stone rubble laid without mortar. Carob, pine, and almond trees surround the house. The terraces are linked together by stone stairways put together by the same method as the walls, a construction system that bears witness to the region's well-qualified stone masons.

The new building for Miró's studio was raised on two of the terraces on the plot. The high curved wall of the upper terrace embraces and shapes a patio that was paved with a mosaic of different kinds of flagstones. The studio is divided into two levels that coincide with the two terraces so that the sculpture patio and the attic are on different levels from the main gallery. This building can be entered from three different levels because the roof has an accessway that gives onto the terrace and rises up above the sculpture patio.

The ground floor houses a small office, a storeroom, and the studio per se. The storeroom is double-height to allow storage of large-format canvases. To the left of the entrance to this room, a smaller room that opens onto a covered terrace contains the painter's collection of folkloric objects, old phonograph records and some books. The studio, also high-ceilinged, has a large window that looks north and that opens out onto the sculpture patio, at the back of the house.

The attic is also open to the studio and used to make prints: lithographs, etchings, or engravings. The windows give a view of the sea, looking out on a group of islands beyond the coastline.

Concrete was used in almost the entire construction, and the wooden molds on which it was poured were studded all over with rivets so that the final finish, painted in white, has a rough texture.

Collaborators: Antonio Ochoa
(Structural Calculations)
Enric Juncosa (Works Supervision)
Location: Palma de Mallorca, Spain
Construction Date: 1975
Photography: Joan Ramon Bonet and Dieter
Bork, Arxiu d'Imatges Fundació
Pilar i Joan Miró (Mallorca),
Pere Planells

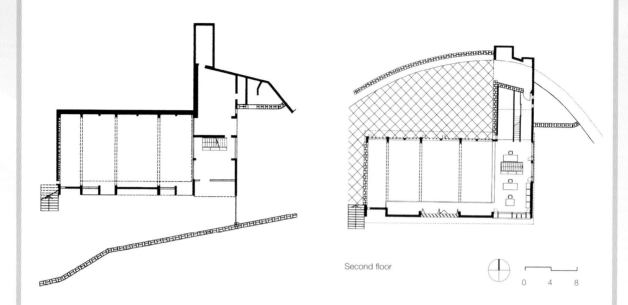

First floor

Second floor

0   4   8

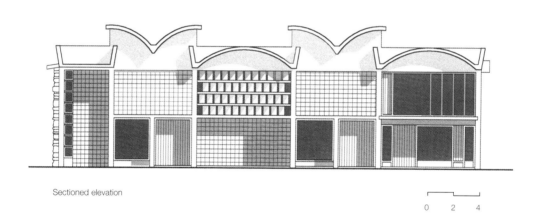

Sectioned elevation

0   2   4

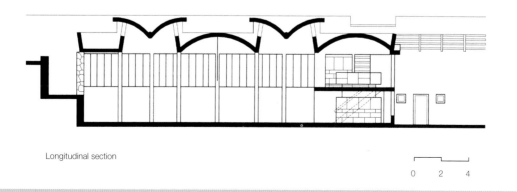

Longitudinal section

0   2   4

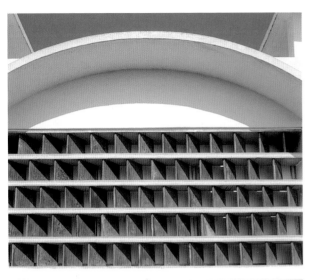

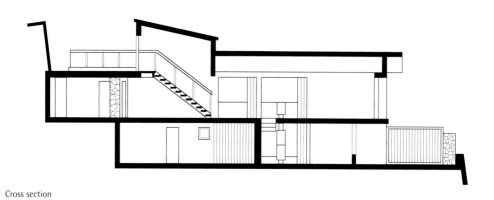

Cross section

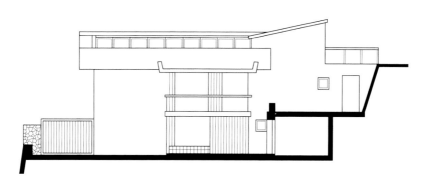

Elevation

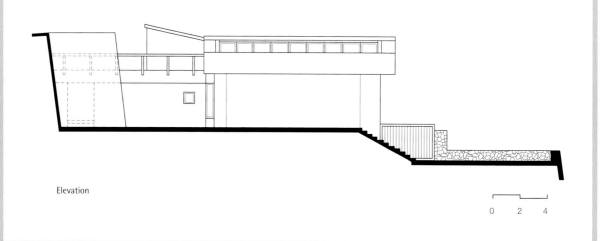

Elevation

0   2   4

Location Maps

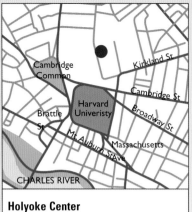

Holyoke Center

Oxford Street, Cambridge,
Massachusetts, USA

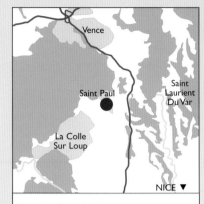

Maeght Foundation

Chemin de Gardette,
Saint-Paul-de-Vence, France

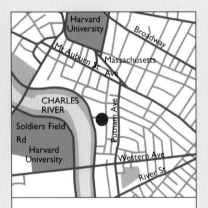

**Apartments
for married students**

Memorial Drive, Cambridge,
Massachusetts, USA

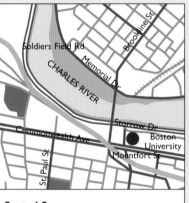

**Central Campus.
Boston University**

Commonwealth Avenue, Boston,
Massachussets, USA

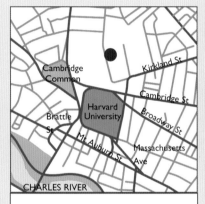

**Science Center.
Harvard University**

Oxford Street, Cambridge,
Massachusetts, USA

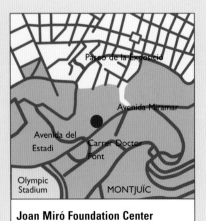

**Joan Miró Foundation Center
of studies in Contemporary Art**

Avenida del Estadi,
Barcelona, Spain

Joan Miró Studio

Joan de Saridakis 29,
Palma de Mallorca, Spain

Chronology of Works

1931	Building with duplex house, Calle Muntaner, Barcelona, Spain.
1934	Roca Jewelry, Paseo de Gracia, Barcelona, Spain. In collaboration with Antonio Bonet.
1935	Weekend houses in Garraf, Barcelona, Spain. In collaboration with Josep Torres-Clavé.
1935	Central Anti-tuberculosis Dispensary, Barcelona, Spain. In collaboration with Josep Torres-Clavé and J. B. Subirana.
1937	The Spain pavilion for the Internacional Exposition, Paris, France. In collaboration with Lluís Lacasa.
1945	Cidade dos Motores, Brasil. With Town Planning Associates.
1948	The new city of Chimbote, Peru. With Town Planning Associates.
1949	Sert house in Locust Valley, Long Island, New York, USA.
1949	Master plan of Medellín, Colombia. With Town Planning Associates.
1951	Master plan of Bogotá, Colombia. With Town Planning Associates
1955-1960	Embassy of the United States, Bagdad, Iraq.
1956-1958	Pilot plan of Havana, Cuba. With Town Planning Associates.
1958	Sert house in Cambridge, Massachusetts, USA.
1958-1966	Holyoke Center, Harvard University, Cambridge, Massachusetts, USA.
1959-1964	Maeght Foundation , Saint-Paul-de-Vence, France.
1960	Center for the Study of World Religions, Harvard University, Cambridge, Massachusetts, USA. With Sert, Jackson & Gourley.
1961	Offices for New England Gas and Electric Association, Cambridge, Massachusetts, USA. With Sert, Jackson & Gourley.
1961	House on the Paseo de la Muralla, Ibiza, Spain.
1962-1964	Apartments for married students, Harvard University, Massachusetts, USA.
1963-1966	Central Campus, University of Boston, Boston, Massachusetts, USA.
1967	University of Guelph, Ontario, Canada. With Sert, Jackson & Associates. In collaboration with Hancock Little Calvert.
1967	Convent Carmel de la Paix, Cluny, France. With Sert, Jackson & Associates.
1968-1973	Les Escales Park Houses, Barcelona, Spain. With Sert, Jackson & Associates.
1968	Houses in Punta Martinet, Ibiza, Spain. With Sert, Jackson & Associates.
1970-1972	Science Center, Harvard University, Massachusetts, USA.
1971	Offices in the building at 44 Brattle Street, Cambridge, Massachusetts, USA. With Sert, Jackson & Associates.
1972	Martin Luther King Elementary School, Cambridge, Massachusetts, USA. With Sert, Jackson & Associates.
1973-1976	Riverview Houses, Yonkers, New York, USA. With Sert, Jackson & Associates.
1973-1976	Roosevelt Island Houses, New York, USA. With Sert, Jackson & Associates.
1975	Joan Miró Foundation. Center of studies in Contemporary Art, Barcelona, Spain.
1975	Studio for Joan Miró, Palma de Mallorca, Spain.
1976	Puerta Catalana, Girona, Spain.

Selected Bibliography

BASTHUND, Knud (1967): *José Luis Sert, architecture, city planning, urban design*, Zürich, Verlagfür Architektur (Artemis).

ROVIRA, Josep M. (2001): *Sert 1901-1983*, Milán, Editorial Electa.

PIZZA, Antonio (1997): *Josep LLuís Sert y el Mediterráneo*, Barcelona, Collegi d'Arquitectes de Barcelona.

COSTA, Xavier and HARTRAY, Guido (1997): *Sert, arquitecto en Nueva York*, Catalogue of an exhibition in the Centre for Contemporary Art of Barcelona (CCCB), Barcelona, Actar.

MARURINO, Edgardo and PARICIO, Ignacio (1983): *Josep Lluís Sert: construcción y arquitectura*, Barcelona, Gustavo Gili.

FREIXA, Jaume (1979): *Josep Lluís Sert*, Barcelona, Gustavo Gili (Estudio Paperback).

Acknowledgments

We would like to thank the useful help of:

Huson Jackson
Jaume Freixa

Salvador Cardona (architect)
Leticia Eguilior
Gomis Family
Marc Ingla i Mas and Claudia Vives-Fierro i Planas
Luis Rodríguez Mori
Antonia de Sert
Toni Mari Torres (architect)